T0130098

The Official Rules for

ZOOM SCHWARTZ PROFIGLIANO

THE OFFICIAL RULES FOR

ZOOM SCHWARTZ PROFIGLIANO

ESHELMAN, OSHEVSKY, GROID, HEGEMAN, COMANECI, NADIA, BOZIT, BOAR, OBIWAN, BEN KENOBE, FREZNIK, WHAT/WHAT, LAGNAF, QUEETH AND KOWALSKI

JON MELZER AND BRUCE HACKETT

Members of the Varsity Beverage Team
of Cleveland and the World

Illustrations by Teresa Lionetti

iUniverse, Inc.
Bloomington

The Official Rules for Zoom Schwartz Profigliano
Eshelman, Oshevsky, Groid, Hegeman, Comaneci, Nadia, Bozit, Boar, Obiwan, Ben Kenobe, Freznik, What/What, LAGNAF, Queeth and Kowalski

DISCLAIMER
In no way do the authors or publishers condone or encourage the abuse of alcoholic beverages. The game described in this book should be played responsibly and by all means can be played with non-alcoholic beverages. In no way is this material intended to promote binge-drinking, alcoholism, underage drinking, hazing, drunk driving, or any other form of alcohol abuse. THE AUTHORS AND/OR PUBLISHERS ASSUME NO LIABILITY OR RESPONSIBILITY, AND SHALL BE HELD HARMLESS, FOR PERSONAL, FINANCIAL OR PROPERTY DAMAGE, PERSONAL INJURY, OR DEATH ARISING, DIRECTLY OR INDIRECTLY, FROM PLAYING THE GAME DESCRIBED IN THIS BOOK. **This publication is intended for entertainment, amusement and novelty purposes only.**

iUniverse books may be ordered through booksellers or by contacting:
iUniverse
1663 Liberty Drive
Bloomington, IN 47403
www.iuniverse.com
1-800-Authors (1-800-288-4677)

Because of the dynamic nature of the Internet, any web addresses or links contained in this book may have changed since publication and may no longer be valid. The views expressed in this work are solely those of the author and do not necessarily reflect the views of the publisher, and the publisher hereby disclaims any responsibility for them.

Any people depicted in stock imagery provided by Thinkstock are models, and such images are being used for illustrative purposes only. Certain stock imagery © Thinkstock.

ISBN: 978-1-4759-9250-2 (sc)
ISBN: 978-1-4759-9251-9 (e)

Printed in the United States of America.
iUniverse rev. date: 06/04/2013

FOREWORD

A long time ago at a private boys school in the suburbs of Cleveland, Ohio, eighteen senior classmates banded together to form a fraternity of sorts called the Varsity Beverage Team (a.k.a., the VB). The VB would periodically have banquets where they wore silly attire, drank, laughed, drank, sang, chanted, drank, roasted each other, and drank. The VB expanded over the years into a group of thirty, and almost four decades later, they still cavort at VB banquets, drinking, laughing, and reminiscing about our past glories. Over the years, one constant has been our affinity for drinking games. We strongly believe that competition and drinking go very well together. In our early, formative years, there probably wasn't a drinking game that we didn't play. Conventional drinking games generally seemed mundane and boring, so we decided to invent a few of our own, the greatest of which was an adaptation of Zoom Schwartz Profigliano. Zoom Schwartz is the greatest drinking game you will ever play. Anyone who has ever played it or has seen it played will agree with this assertion. It is simply referred to as "The Game."

The VB has grown older, and many of us now have adult kids. Many of the next generation, the self-proclaimed VB2Gs, have observed their old men playing The Game and, being intrigued, have asked to join in the frivolity. Besides being challenging and fun, The Game is also quite addictive. After learning the first few calls and playing with their VB Dads until the beer ran out, they clamored for more of the game. In fact, they implored us to write down the rules so they could learn all the calls and the beautiful nuances of The Game. This was something we had intended to do for years, but the VB2Gs gave us the inspiration we needed to get off our asses and write down the rules.

The Game is extraordinarily complex but can be learned gradually, in stages. The deeper one gets into the game, the more enjoyable it becomes. We encourage you to learn not just all the calls, but also the details of the accompanying rules and terminology.

So collect a group of friends, stockpile massive quantities of the beverage of your choice, grab this rule book, and start playing. You will laugh till it hurts. We promise it will be the most fun you've ever had with your clothes on.

THE RULES FOR
ZOOM SCHWARTZ PROFIGLIANO

Eshelman, Oshevsky, Groid, Hegeman, Comaneci, Nadia, Bozit, Boar, Obiwan, Ben Kenobe, Freznik, What/What, LAGNAF, Queeth and Kowalski

"Of course, we all know how to play the game ..."

But, of course, that is absolutely *not* true. Most people have *no* idea how to play this game. Some people will never know. But a brave few are eager to learn. And for those people, the Rules Committee of the Varsity Beverage Team is, at long last, putting down on paper the official rules of this hallowed game for future generations to learn and enjoy.

The genesis of Zoom Schwartz is somewhat murky. There is evidence to suggest the game was born in the 1940s on a college campus in California, as a diversion designed to challenge beer drinkers to use their minds while pickling their minds at the same time. It was known only as "Zoom Schwartz Profigliano." Three calls. That's it. And they meant pretty much the same thing then that they do now.

PART 1: ZOOM SCHWARTZ PROFIGLIANO AND BASIC RULES

A Few Preliminaries

We have found that the optimum number of players for a really quality game of Zoom Schwartz is between four and eight. Once you have more than eight, it can still be fun and entertaining, but it's harder to see who's zoomin' whom, and who's elbowing whom, and rules enforcement gets a bit lax.

Zoom Schwartz can be an indoor or outdoor game. Players may sit around a table, they may sit on chairs with no table, or they may stand in a circle. They may even dog-paddle in a circle in a swimming pool. Any of these are acceptable.

Any beverage can be used when playing the game, but beer is the most typical. For purposes of this document, we will assume that beer is the beverage of choice. You should ensure there is enough beer on hand to keep the game going. Typically, all players should use the same sized vessel—mug, bottle, can, cup, whatever—as long as everyone starts with the same amount of beer (usually twelve ounces). This matters once you're at the point of chugging, which we'll discuss later.

Throughout this document, all pronouns are of the male gender. Women should take no offense at this; most players are indeed male. But there have been some highly qualified female players over the years, and women are every bit as welcome to learn and play as men. Come on, we double dare you.

Starting the Game

Each round is begun by saying the Creed: "Of course, we all know how to play the game Zoom Schwartz Profigliano …" (up to whatever call you choose to include; there are eighteen in all). Then all players take a sip. Anyone may choose to start the first round of a game of Zoom Schwartz. From then on, the player who makes a mistake and is called for it starts the next round.

Whenever a new player enters the game, he starts the next round. Note: a new player may not enter the game when a player is pending a chug. The new player must wait until that player's fate is determined. (He makes an infraction and must chug, or he is vindicated.) This will all be discussed in more detail later. A glossary of terms is provided at the end of the document.

Zoom

"Zoom" starts the game. The player who starts the round looks directly at another player, any player, and says, "Zoom." Very basic. (Later on, you'll learn there are other calls that are allowable for starting the game, but for now, "Zoom" starts the game.)

The player who was Zoomed then has three options:

1) He can Zoom another player, any other player. Important note: he can *never* Zoom the player who Zoomed him. That is very embarrassing and grounds for an immediate chug.

Schwartz

2) He can look back at the player who Zoomed him and say, "Schwartz." This is like a "ricochet" that sends it back to the player who Zoomed him. Schwartz can be used as a ricochet to most calls, not just Zoom.

Profigliano

3) He can look *away* from the player who Zoomed him and say, "Profigliano." This has the same effect as a Schwartz: It sends it back to the person who Zoomed him, but with a "head fake." Profigliano can be used as a head-fake ricochet to most calls, not just Zoom or Schwartz.

So what happens next? The next player has the same three options. He can look at someone new and say, "Zoom"; he can look directly at the player who sent the call to him and say, "Schwartz"; or he can look away from the player who sent the call to him and say, "Profigliano."

Typically, beginners find themselves using Zoom a lot because it's always easier to just Zoom someone new, but players who learn to master Schwartz and Profigliano in a fast-paced game will be ready sooner to introduce more calls to the game. Remember, we still have fifteen to go!

Players jockey and spar, on and on, until someone makes a mistake. In Zoom Schwartz, we call this an infraction. And that's when the elbows start to fly.

Elbows and Resolving Disputes

We believe it is rude to point—with your finger, anyway. If you use a finger to point at anybody or anything at any time during a game, you will be called for Pointing, which requires a penalty drink. We much prefer to point with our elbow when we want to accuse someone of something. When a player has made an incorrect call or has responded when it's not his turn to respond, any other player may throw an elbow at the offending player and state the reason why he believes an infraction has been made.

Sometimes, it's obvious to all, and the offending player sheepishly takes his penalty sip and begins the next round. In fact, sometimes it's so obvious to the offending player that he takes his penalty sip even before any elbows are thrown!

But sometimes there is disagreement as to whether an infraction has been made. This usually occurs when the offending player has *failed* to respond in "a reasonable amount of time." With beginning players, enforcement is usually more lenient, as they are still learning the game. With more advanced players, enforcement can and should be more rigorous. It's really at the discretion of those playing. But essentially, if *two* or more players point their elbows at a player who is supposed to respond but has not done so in "a reasonable amount of time," that player is considered guilty of Hesitancy, which is an infraction.

If the offending player disagrees, he may challenge the ruling by calling for a vote of all players. All players extend their arms into the circle with a thumb stuck out to the side (neutral position) as they wait to hear the terms of the vote. The offending player then selects which player he believes must drink if he wins the vote, for *someone* must drink. For example, if Rock and Hack throw elbows at Abood for a late response, and Abood disagrees, he can call for a vote. He may select Rock or Hack as the player who must drink if Abood wins the challenge. He then says, "Up, I drink, down, Hack drinks. Ready, Vote!" Each player then votes up or down with his thumb, and the loser must drink. If any player finds himself as the only one who voted a certain way, he must drink *two* sips.

Multiple Consecutive Infractions and "Shoupies"

Even the best player dreads finding himself in the position of making two or more infractions in a row. First, it's embarrassing, but second, he risks having to chug his beer if he makes a *third* consecutive infraction. A player who is having a really bad day and keeps making consecutive infractions will have to chug again when he reaches *five* straight infractions, and *seven* straight infractions, and then every infraction thereafter.

Players who have made two (or four, or six, etc.) consecutive infractions and must chug if they make another are considered "Pending a chug." Advanced players will often prey on these players with various strategies designed to compel them to finish what's left of their beer and open a brand-new one, thus requiring chugging a full beer if that third (or fifth, or seventh, etc.) infraction in a row is made.

Whenever another player makes an infraction, the player who had been pending is Vindicated: He now has zero infractions outstanding. We don't like seeing a player who is pending a chug being saved by another player who makes an infraction. Therefore, a player who makes an infraction when another player is pending a chug is guilty of a Shoupie. It's an additional one-sip penalty on top of the penalty drink for the infraction. However, this type of infraction is *accumulative* over the course of the day's game. (A "day" is defined as the period of partying between two nights' sleep. For example, you are not absolved of your Shoupies at midnight if the game is still ongoing.) If a player accumulates three Shoupies in one day, the penalty is a chug. If he accumulates five Shoupies, that's another chug, and again if he reaches seven Shoupies (although this is pretty rare).

* * *

So, are you with us so far? Can you handle these basic rules of Zoom Schwartz Profigliano?

If you're hopelessly confused, stop now. Return to your home. Take up knitting. Go play checkers or something. You'll never make it through Zoom Schwartz Profigliano Eshelman Oshevsky Groid Hegeman Comaneci Nadia Bozit Boar Obiwan Ben Kenobe Freznik What/What LAGNAF Queeth and Kowalski.

But perhaps you're smarter than the average Neanderthal or Steelers fan. You've mastered the simple basics and are ready to learn additional calls. You're ready to go beyond the crude fundamentals the Varsity Beverage Team inherited from some previous incarnation and learn the rules added by the VB in their college years and beyond, which make the game far more challenging and satisfying.

Very well, then. Here we go …

PART 2: THE REST
OF THE CREED

———————◆◆◆———————

Eshelman and Oshevsky

These two calls were added at the same time because they complement each other. When a player says, "Eshelman," the player on his *left* must respond. When a player says, "Oshevsky," the player on his *right* must respond. A player saying "Eshelman" may not look at his Eshelman, and a player saying "Oshevsky" may not look at his Oshevsky. You must look anywhere but at the Eshelman, or the Oshevsky. It's basically the same "head fake" rule used for Profigliano.

So you now have *five* options: 1) Zoom someone new. 2) Schwartz the player who sent the call to you. 3) Profigliano (head fake) the player who sent the call to you. 4) Eshelman the player on your left (but don't look at him). 5) Oshevsky the player on your right (but don't look at him).

As the VB was developing the game, we got very, very good at playing the game with just these five calls: Zoom, Schwartz, Profigliano, Eshelman, and Oshevsky. But we soon discovered if you're really good, you make very few infractions, and you might be sitting there a long time between sips, getting thirsty. In Zoom Schwartz, players are only permitted to take sips from their beers when compelled to. Taking a random sip is considered Drinking Out of Turn. The penalty, of course, is another sip.

9

A player who simply cannot wait for a legitimate opportunity to drink will sometimes take a random sip, throw an elbow at himself, say, "Drinking Out of Turn," and take a penalty sip as well. What a great game!

To prevent anarchy and an epidemic of Drinking Out of Turn, we saw the need to add a call that would bring more permissible drinking into the game. Which brings us to Kowalski.

Kowalski

This might be the most important call in the game. When a player says, "Kowalski," the action in the game temporarily halts while *all* players take a sip from their beers. Good players are delighted to finally have a chance to sip their beer, and it gives lesser players a break, as they can momentarily collect their thoughts and determine their next move.

A player may *always* say "Kowalski" in response to any other call. And Kowalski is also an allowable choice for starting a round. And it doesn't matter who you're looking at when you say Kowalski. Just say, "Kowalski," and everything stops, and everyone takes a sip. Gotta love this call. Use it frequently.

The player who calls Kowalski is responsible for making the next call. He now has *six* options: 1) Zoom someone new. 2) Schwartz the player who sent the call to him. 3) Profigliano the player who sent the call to him. 4) Eshelman the player on his left. 5) Oshevsky the player on his right. 6) Say "Kowalski" again.

Obviously, the introduction of Kowalski exponentially increases the amount of drinking in the game. Consequently, the use of Kowalski can be a diabolical strategic weapon for the better players as well as a "help line" for the average players. We'll discuss these subtleties later.

From this point on, there are twelve calls yet to be added. As these calls are added, Kowalski always brings up the rear as the final call of the Creed.

Groid and Hegeman (pronounced "Heggaman")

Once again, the VB added two calls at once because they complement each other, much like Eshelman and Oshevsky. But here's the difference: with Groid and Hegeman, a player *becomes that call* for the duration of the round. An explanation:

Groid is the player who starts a given round. He remains the Groid for the duration of the round. Anytime a player says, "Groid," the Groid must respond. A player saying "Groid" must not look at the Groid (more head-faking). Looking at the Groid while saying "Groid" is a three-sip infraction. Also, the Groid is forbidden from using the term Groid in that round because he *is* the Groid for that round. If he "Groids" himself, he is responsible for a three-sip penalty.

Hegeman is the first person Zoomed in a given round. For instance, let's say Rock Zooms Yard to start the round. Rock is now the Groid for the round, and Yard is now the Hegeman for the duration of that round. Anytime a player says, "Hegeman," the Hegeman must respond. A player saying "Hegeman" must not look at the Hegeman. Looking at the Hegeman while saying "Hegeman" is a three-sip penalty. Also, the Hegeman is prohibited from using the term Hegeman in that round because he *is* the Hegeman for that round. If he "Hegemans" himself, he must take a three-sip penalty.

With each new round, there is a new Groid (unless the Groid made the last infraction and must start again). With each round, there is also a new Hegeman.

A player now has *eight* options: 1) Zoom someone new. 2) Schwartz the player who sent the call to him. 3) Profigliano the player who sent the call to him. 4) Eshelman the player on his left. 5) Oshevsky the player on his right. 6) Groid the player who started the round. 7) Hegeman the first person Zoomed in the round. 8) Say "Kowalski."

Comaneci (pronounced "Comaneech") and Nadia

In the summer of 1976, at the Montreal Olympics, Romania's fourteen-year-old wunderkind Nadia Comaneci was not only the first gymnast to score a perfect 10 in an Olympic event, she tallied SEVEN perfect 10s during the competition. We thought this made her worthy of inclusion in our game.

During the Olympics, when commentators asked her how to pronounce her name properly, she replied like a dutiful little Communist Bloc girl: "Comaneci, Nadia" (last name first). So we adopted it that way.

Essentially, Comaneci and Nadia are a two-player version of Kowalski. When a player says, "Comaneci," it's like a Schwartz, because the player who sent the call to him must respond, and he *must* respond with "Nadia." Then everyone drinks, just like a Kowalski. Note: like Kowalski, it doesn't matter who you're looking at when you say, "Comaneci" or "Nadia."

If, after a player says, "Comaneci," the player who is supposed to respond doesn't say, "Nadia" (or says something other than "Nadia"), that's a major infraction and the player must take a penalty sip and start a new round.

An important difference from Kowalski: the player who says "Nadia" does *not* get to make the next call. The person who said "Comaneci" makes the next call. Essentially, the player saying "Nadia" is a pawn. If the player who said "Nadia" attempts to make the next call, that's a major infraction. He must take a sip and start a new round.

You now have *nine* options: 1) Zoom someone new. 2) Schwartz the player who sent the call to you. 3) Profigliano the player who sent the call to you. 4) Eshelman the player on your left. 5) Oshevsky the player on your right. 6) Groid the player who started the round. 7) Hegeman the first player Zoomed in the round. 8) Say "Comaneci" (and the person who sent the call to you must say, "Nadia"). 9) Say "Kowalski."

Bozit (pronounced "Bozeet")

At this point in the development of the game, players must remember who started the round (the Groid) and who was first Zoomed (Hegeman). Now, with Bozit, players will be required to remember the Groid of the *previous* round: that's the Bozit. So when you're the Groid of a given round, once that round ends, you must remember that you are now the Bozit for the next round. (Note: if you make an infraction in the round where you're the Groid, then you're going to be the Groid *and* the Bozit in the next round. Gotta keep your shit together at this point, as you will be pending a chug.)

As with the Groid and the Hegeman, players may not look at the Bozit when saying, "Bozit." To do so is a three-sip penalty. And the Bozit may not say "Bozit" in that round because he *is* the Bozit for that round. A player who "Bozits" himself owes a three-sip penalty. Also, as with Groid and Hegeman, the Bozit changes with every round (unless the same player keeps making infractions).

Also, Bozit is an allowable choice with which to begin a round (except the very first round, because there has been no previous round yet).

You now have *ten* options: 1) Zoom someone new. 2) Schwartz the player who sent the call to you. 3) Profigliano the player who sent the call to you. 4) Eshelman the player on your left. 5) Oshevsky the player on your right. 6) Groid the player who started the round. 7) Hegeman the first player Zoomed in the round. 8) Say "Comaneci" (and the player who sent the call to you must say, "Nadia"). 9) Bozit the player who started the previous round. 10) Say "Kowalski."

Boar

This may be the most wonderfully inventive call we've come up with. When a player looks at a player and says "Boar" for the first time in a round, that player becomes the Boar. Thereafter, whenever any other player says, "Boar," the Boar must respond, just as with Groid, Hegeman, and Bozit. Players may not look at the Boar when saying, "Boar."

But here's the creative part of this call: the player who has become the Boar has the power to *transfer* the Boar to another player merely by looking at him and saying, "Boar." Example: Rock looks at Hack and says, "Boar." Hack is now the Boar for the round ... until Hack chooses to look at another player (let's say Abood) and say, "Boar." Now Abood is the Boar for the rest of the round ... until *he* decides to transfer it again to another player. Keeping track of who the Boar is when it is transferred multiple times is obviously quite a challenge!

Also, Boar is an allowable call with which to begin a round.

You now have *eleven* options: 1) Zoom someone new. 2) Schwartz the player who sent the call to you. 3) Profigliano the player who sent the call to you. 4) Eshelman the player on your left. 5) Oshevsky the player on your right. 6) Groid the player who started the round. 7) Hegeman the first player Zoomed in the round. 8) Say "Comaneci" (and the player who sent the call to you must say, "Nadia"). 9) Bozit the player who started the previous round. 10) Say "Boar" to any player (on first usage), or Boar the player who is the Boar, or transfer the Boar to another player (if you're the Boar). 11) Say "Kowalski."

Obiwan and Ben Kenobe

Obiwan is the player seated to the *left* of the Groid. Ben Kenobe is the player seated to the *right* of the Groid. Therefore, as soon as someone starts a round and the identity of the Groid is established, the identity of the Obiwan and the Ben Kenobe are also established. These players retain these designations for the rest of the round, just as with the Groid, Hegeman, and Bozit. Again, players may not look at the Obiwan when saying, "Obiwan," and they may not look at the Ben Kenobe when they say, "Ben Kenobe." The Obiwan may not "Obiwan" himself, and the Ben Kenobe may not "Ben Kenobe" himself. Any of these infractions are three-sip penalties.

Also, Obiwan and Ben Kenobe are allowable calls with which to begin a round.

You now have *thirteen* options: 1) Zoom someone new. 2) Schwartz the player who sent the call to you. 3) Profigliano the player who sent the call to you. 4) Eshelman the player on your left. 5) Oshevsky the player on your right. 6) Groid the player who started the round. 7) Hegeman the first player Zoomed in the round. 8) Say "Comaneci" (and the player who sent the call to you must say, "Nadia"). 9) Bozit the player who started the previous round. 10) Say "Boar" to another player (on first usage), or Boar the player who is the Boar, or transfer the Boar to another player (if you're the Boar). 11) Obiwan the player to the left of the Groid. 12) Ben Kenobe the player to the right of the Groid. 13) Say "Kowalski."

Freznik

This call was originated to bring still more drinking into the game, but in a more targeted way. When a player looks at another player and says, "Freznik," there is a temporary stop in the action (as with Kowalski or with Comaneci and Nadia), but only these two players may drink. The person who said "Freznik" then makes the next call.

The use of Freznik is often used when a player is pending but has only one or two sips remaining in his beer. When that player is Frezniked once or twice, he is expected to have finished that beer and must open a new one. If he makes the next infraction, he must now chug the new full beer instead of the nearly empty beer he had been holding. This is a brutally effective strategy to combat lightweights. (Kowalski and Comaneci/Nadia are also effective weapons used to drain a pending player's beer before "going for the chugular.")

Also, Freznik is an allowable call with which to begin a round.

What/What

This call adds a whole new degree of difficulty to the game. The What/What call is actually two calls, but they must be used together at the same time. A player using this call looks at Player A and says, "What," and then looks at Player B and says, "What." It is Player B's responsibility to respond, and he must send the call to either Player A or the player who said, "What/What." He can use any call he wishes as long as he sends the call to one of those two players.

For example, if Rock says "What" to Yard and then "What" to Abood, it is Abood who must respond. He must send the call to either Rock or Yard in one way or another. Abood has a number of options: he can Schwartz Rock, he can Profigliano Rock, he can Zoom Yard, he can What/What either Rock or Yard, he can use Eshelman or Oshevsky (if Rock or Yard are on his left or right), he can use Groid or Hegeman or Bozit or Boar or Obiwan or Ben Kenobe *if* Rock or Yard are so designated in that round, he can Freznik Rock or Yard, he can Comaneci Rock (who must then say, "Nadia"), or he can say, "Kowalski." If he chooses Kowalski, he must still send it to Rock or Yard on the next call. Sending the call to anyone other than Rock or Yard is a major infraction.

What/What is an allowable call with which to begin a round.

LAGNAF (Let's All Get Naked and Fuck)

This is an ancillary call to What/What. The LAGNAF is the player who is the first What of the first What/What called in a given round. The LAGNAF remains the LAGNAF for the rest of the round. Players may not look at the LAGNAF when saying, "LAGNAF," and the LAGNAF may not say "LAGNAF" in that round because he *is* the LAGNAF in that round. These infractions incur three-sip penalties. Also, players who say "LAGNAF" when no LAGNAF has yet been established (because What/What has not yet been used in a round) are guilty of a major infraction.

Queeth

This is another ancillary call in the What/What family. The Queeth is the player who is the most *recent* first What in the round. Therefore, the Queeth changes each time the What/What call is made in a given round.

Example: in the first use of What/What in the round, Abood says "What" to Hack and then "What" to Rock. Hack is now the LAGNAF for the duration of the round. He is *also* the Queeth and will remain so until the What/What call is used again, at which point a new Queeth is established.

Players may not look at the Queeth when saying, "Queeth," and the Queeth may not say "Queeth" at that point because he *is* the Queeth at that point. Those are three-sip penalties. Also, players who say "Queeth" when no Queeth has yet been established (because What/What has not yet been used in a round) are guilty of a major infraction.

* * *

So now you know the entire Creed. All eighteen calls! Congratulations, you are now a Graduate Level player. Now you know that you have *seventeen* options when it's your turn to respond (no one can choose to say, "Nadia," remember): 1) Zoom someone new. 2) Schwartz the player who sent the call to you. 3) Profigliano the player who sent the call to you. 4) Eshelman the player on your left. 5) Oshevsky the player on your right. 6) Groid the player who started the round. 7) Hegeman the first player Zoomed in the round. 8) Say "Comaneci" (and the player who sent the call to you must say, "Nadia"). 9) Bozit the player who started the previous round. 10) Say "Boar" to another player (on first usage), or Boar the player who is the Boar, or transfer the Boar to another player (if you're the Boar). 11) Obiwan the player to the left of the Groid. 12) Ben Kenobe the player to the right of the Groid. 13) Freznik any player. 14) Say "What" to one player and "What" to another player. 15) LAGNAF the first What of the first What/What in the round (if What/What has been used in the round). 16) Queeth the first What of the most recent What/What in the round (if What/What has been used in the round). 17) Say "Kowalski."

(Remember, though: if a player uses What/What and looks at you on the second What, you *don't* have all seventeen options available to you. You may use only those options that will send the call to the player who said, "What/What," or to the first What.)

At this point, you may know all the calls of the Creed and their meaning, but there are several additional rules you must learn in order to become a Master of Zoom Schwartz.

And here we go.

PART 3:
ADDITIONAL RULES

————◆—◆—◆————

Major and Minor Infractions

Every round of Zoom ends with someone making a *major* infraction, taking a sip, and beginning the next round. In some rounds, there are also *minor* infractions. For example, Hack says, "Oshevsky." Rock, seated to Hack's right, responds, "Eshelman." Abood, seated to Rock's right, then makes a response (incorrectly, since it's Hack's turn). Hack responds correctly, but *after* Abood has responded out of turn. Abood has made the major infraction, has "one on him," and starts the next round. But Hack has a minor infraction. Even though it was his turn to respond, he did so after the major infraction was made, and he must take a penalty drink for that. No big deal, just a small punishment to fit a small crime.

But it is a big deal if Hack has a major infraction on him when he commits the minor. If that happens, Hack retains his major infraction into the next round. If he should make a major infraction in that round, he would now have two majors and be pending a chug.

It's an even bigger deal if Hack has two majors on him when he commits a minor. If that happens, he is *not* vindicated and retains his two infractions into the next round and is pending a chug.

Other situations requiring a penalty drink that may occur during a round include pointing with your finger, drinking out of turn, or saying the word "what" at any time other than when actually using the What/What call.

(For this last one, most players learn to merely substitute the word "which" for "what" in conversation to avoid this infraction. Advanced players will sometimes quickly say something quietly or mumble in an attempt to get someone to say, "What?" in response. Watch out for this trick, it's an easy trap to fall for.)

"Time Out" and "Ni Emit"

If you must temporarily leave the game—to use the bathroom, to fetch another beer, to take a phone call, to argue with your lady about how drunk you're getting—you *must* make the perpendicular T sign with your hands, roll your hands in a spinning motion, and declare, "Time Out!" Conversely, when you return to the game, you must reverse what you did: spin your hands in the opposite direction, make the T sign, and declare, "Ni Emit!" (That's "Time In" backwards.)

If you leave the game without calling Time Out, other players can proceed as if you're still there, send a call to where you were sitting, and then call you for the major infraction of failing to respond. When you return to the game, you will be informed of your error and must take your penalty drink. But you must call Time In ("Ni Emit") first. Any penalty drinks taken while you have a Time Out do not count, and you must take them again after you call Time In.

Note: this is why, when you call a Time Out, it's best to make certain one or two other players hear and see you call Time Out so you won't be charged with failing to call a Time Out.

When you return to the game after a Time Out, you must wait until a round is completed before calling Time In. You cannot (and would be foolish to) return in the middle of a round because you won't know who the Groid is, or Hegeman, or Boar, and so on.

"1-2-3-4-5"

Advanced Zoom players get exasperated when there are needless delays in the game. A high-spirited, well-played game can lose its momentum when a player gets chatty or forgets it is his turn to start the round. On those occasions, an impatient player may say, "1-2-3-4-5," and throw an elbow at the tardy player. The player must drink for Delay of Game, unless he was able to quickly start the Creed before the player completed counting to 5. If the tardy player is still paying no attention to his responsibility to start the round, the impatient player can then say, "1-2-3-4-5 Double," and the tardy player now owes two sips. The other player might even then say, "1-2-3-4-5 Triple," and now the tardy player owes three sips. At that point, the tardy player may say "Time Out" for a moment to halt the accumulation of penalties, then call Time In again, take his penalty sips, and begin the round.

"1-2-5 Double, 1-2-5 Triple, 1-2-5 Quadruple"

Advanced Zoom Schwartz players who want to keep the momentum going have another tactic available to them. When a player has made an infraction and multiple elbows are pointed at him, he must either take his penalty sip(s) or contest the charge by calling for a vote. If he hesitates, any aggressive player who has thrown an elbow may say, "1-2-5 Double." The offending player now must take two sips instead of one. The aggressive player may go on to say, "1-2-5 Triple," "1-2-5 Quadruple," and so forth, until the offending player either calls Time Out or starts sipping his accrued penalties.

Important: any penalty sips taken during a Time Out do *not* count. If a player foolishly drinks his penalty sips with a Time Out, he must then call Time In and take his penalty sips *again*.

Undue Stoppage

A player who stops the action of the game for any invalid reason is guilty of Undue Stoppage, which is a major infraction. If a player throws an elbow and accuses a player of an infraction that turns out to be incorrect, that's an "Asshole Call," which is the most common form of Undue Stoppage. If a player blurts out any random comment unrelated to the action of the game (like "Check out the cleavage on that girl" or "Hey, the house is on fire"), he is guilty of Undue Stoppage.

Spillage

As in any drinking game, or even when just hanging out, spilling your beer is a messy inconvenience for all players that must be punished. The penalty is negotiable. It stands to reason if you spill a full beer, you should have to drink a full beer. If you spill just a little, perhaps you drink only a little. Majority rules.

Slurrage

There will be times when a player tries to say the Creed too fast or loses his place, or is now drunk and is tripping over his words. If, in the opinion of any player who throws an elbow, the Creed has not been properly enunciated, the offending player must drink and start again. If there's a dispute, vote on it, but this is not an infraction, because the round's action has not actually begun, so take your sip like a man and try again, mush mouth. If a player slurs the name of a call while responding in midgame, any other player can throw an elbow and call him on it. For example, if a player changes his mind in midresponse and says something like, "Sh-zoom," he's not likely to get away with it. In this case, it would be a major infraction.

Wandering Calls

When a player uses a call that requires looking directly at a player (Zoom, Schwartz, Boar on first usage or transfer, Freznik, or What/What), he must "lock on" to the player to whom he's sending the call. Advanced players love to quickly look away *after* making their calls in the hope the player wasn't paying attention and can then be called for failure to respond. But he must "lock on" before looking away. Any roving or wandering head or eye movement while saying the call makes it difficult or impossible to determine who's being Zoomed (or whatever) and must be discouraged. If a player feels there has been blatant wandering, he can throw an elbow and challenge. This is a major infraction because the round has officially begun, so there will likely be spirited disagreement about this. Majority vote rules.

Failure to Drink

When a player is not paying attention when the Creed is recited and all players drink, he is vulnerable to this phenomenon. The player who said the Creed may have noticed the player who wasn't paying attention, and he preys on him by starting the game by Zooming him. When that player responds to being Zoomed, he can immediately be called for Failure to Drink, because he never drank for the Creed. Essentially, he's playing the round illegally and has stopped the game. It's a major infraction because the game has begun when the infraction was made.

Drinking Out of Turn

This was discussed earlier, so just to recap: a player may take a sip only upon completion of the Creed, when he has made an infraction or otherwise incurred a penalty drink, or when he has been "Kowalskied," "Frezniked," or "Comaneci/Nadia-ed." A player who takes an unauthorized random sip is guilty of Drinking Out of Turn, which requires (what else?) a penalty drink.

Beer Check

When a player is pending, any player may demand a beer check of that player's can, mug, bottle, or cup to determine how much beer remains. This is to prevent lightweights from getting away with paying a penalty chug with only a couple of sips remaining in their beers. Typically, if the pending player's beer is found to be more than half empty, the checker tells the players, "Kowalski (or Freznik or Comaneci/Nadia) him to death!"

Offensive Strategies

Diversionary Elbow

Advanced players love to occasionally throw an elbow at a player who has not made an infraction. It's a great way of intimidating him into responding when it's not his turn, which would be a major infraction. (If you choose to try this tactic, be sure to remain silent as you throw your elbow, because if you make a false accusation and action is stopped, you'll likely be guilty of an Asshole Call.)

Provoking Slurrage

The player who is reciting the Creed to start a round may notice a player is a bit slow to take his end-of-Creed sip. The starting player can quickly Zoom that player while he is still struggling to swallow his mouthful of beer. The player will either try to make a call with beer in his mouth and almost certainly end up guilty of slurrage, or he'll attempt to swallow the beer in his mouth before responding and risk being called for hesitancy. Either result would be a major infraction.

Loading Up a Player on Calls

In a round where a player is pending, he will be both the Groid and the Bozit. Advanced players can make it even more difficult on the player who's pending by also making that player the LAGNAF, the Queeth, and the Boar, at least for a while. The pending player would then have a whole plate of stuff he must remember, increasing the odds he'll make a third infraction and have to chug.

Using the Creed to "Sucker" a Player

The player who is about to begin a round might notice another player isn't paying full attention to the game. The starting player can start the Creed by saying, at a more subdued volume, "Of course, we all know how to play the game …," and then look right at the inattentive player and say, "Zoom!" Sometimes that player is caught off guard, thinks the Creed has been said while he wasn't watching and he's being Zoomed to start the game, and is tricked into responding out of turn. It's not a major infraction, because the action of the round hasn't officially begun until the Creed is completed, but it is a penalty drink, and it's always fun to nail someone for not paying attention.

Acceptable Calls to Start the Game

To review, these eight calls are allowable calls with which to begin a round:

Zoom
Bozit
Boar
Obiwan
Ben Kenobe
Freznik
What/What
Kowalski

GLOSSARY OF TERMS

In conclusion, we have included a Glossary of Terms as a handy reference when you're learning the intricacies of the game, or when you're teaching the game to newcomers. We hope this proves helpful.

Asshole Call: Unjustified elbow that stops the game

Beer Check: Inspecting a player's beer to determine how much remains when a chug is pending

Ben Kenobe: The person to the right of the Groid

Boar: The player so designated on first use, and transferable by that player thereafter

Bozit: The Groid of the previous round

Chug: The prompt finishing of the player's remaining beverage

Comaneci Nadia: A two-man Kowalski call after which all players drink

Creed: The full name of the game recited at the beginning of each round

Delay of Game: When a player takes too long to start the next round

Drinking Out of Turn: Taking an unauthorized drink

Elbow: Used to accuse a player of an infraction or other penalty drink

Eshelman: The player to your left

Failure to Drink: When a player doesn't drink for the Creed but responds to a call

Freznik: A personal Kowalski between two players

Groid: The player who starts the round

Hegeman: The first player Zoomed in the round

Hesitancy: When a player fails to respond in a reasonable amount of time and draws two or more elbows from other players; major infraction

Kowalski: Action temporarily stops as all players drink; player who said, "Kowalski," makes next call

LAGNAF: The first What of the first What/What of the round

Major Infraction: A mistake that stops the game or is called by two or more players' elbows during the course of the game; guilty party drinks and starts the next round

Minor Infraction: A mistake made during a round incurred after the major infraction; guilty party takes a penalty drink and retains any previous majors

Ni Emit: Used when a player with a Time Out is ready to rejoin the game; player must spin hands and make the T sign while saying, "Ni Emit" ("Time In" backwards)

Obiwan: The person to the left of the Groid

Oshevsky: The player to your right

Penalty Drink: A required drink resulting from making a Major or Minor Infraction (including Asshole Call, Hesitancy, Undue Stoppage, Failure to Drink), Drinking Out of Turn, Slurrage, Spillage, Pointing, Shoupie, Delay of Game, being the only one voting a certain way, and saying "what" other than as part of a What/What call

Pending: A player who is at risk of chugging if he makes the next major infraction

Pointing: Using your finger to indicate anything at any time during the game

Profigliano: A "head-fake" that sends the call back to the player who sent it to you

Queeth: The first What of the most recent What/What in the round

Schwartz: A "ricochet" that sends the call back to the player who sent it to you

Shoupie: An accumulated infraction made when a player vindicates a pending player

Slurrage: Unacceptable mispronunciation of the Creed or of a call during the round

Spillage: Spilling one's beer

Time Out: Used when a player must temporarily leave the game; player must make the T sign and spin hands while saying, "Time Out"

Undue Stoppage: Any action that stops the game but is determined to be unjustified

Vindication: When a player who was pending a chug is saved and now has zero infractions

Vote: Thumbs-up, thumbs-down consensus of all players when an alleged infraction is being disputed

Wandering: When a player fails to "lock on" to a player when using a call requiring looking directly at a player (Zoom, Schwartz, Boar on first usage or when transferring, Freznik, What/What)

What/What: Player A says "What" to Player B and "What" to Player C; Player C must respond and must send the call to either Player A or B

Zoom: Initial call in the basic game; a player looks directly at a player (never Zoom a Zoom)

Faithfully submitted,
The VB Rules Committee
Bruce "Hack" Hackett, Jon "Rock" Melzer, Barney "Yard" Shirreffs, and Chris Abood

This document is dedicated to the memory of one of the game's creators and very best players: Sir Michelob of Canterbury.

Now & Then

Jon "Rock" Melzer is one of the original members of the Varsity Beverage Team (VB). He was involved in the development of new calls and nuances of Zoom Schwartz Profigliano. He lives in New England and Florida.

Bruce "Hack" Hackett is also one of the original members of the VB. He is an accomplished player of the game and was also involved in its development. He lives in Southern California.

Printed in the United States
By Bookmasters